Machine Embroidered
Seascapes

Alison Holt

First published in paperback 2014

Search Press Limited
Wellwood, North Farm Road,
Tunbridge Wells, Kent TN2 3DR

First published in hardback 2012

ISBN PB: 978-1-78221-114-3
ISBN HB: 978-1-84448-684-7

Suppliers
For details of suppliers, please visit the Search Press
website: www.searchpress.com.

Publisher's note
All the step-by-step photographs in this book feature
the author, Alison Holt, demonstrating machine
embroidery. No models have been used.

Please note that some of the finished embroideries are
reproduced slightly larger than actual size to add clarity
to the stitching.

Printed in China

Acknowledgements

I have had lots of encouragement and support while
writing this book and would like to mention a few
people who have really made a difference.

A huge thank you to my son, Tom, for his much-
valued creative input; to my good friends Keith and Jill
for the perfect holiday, where I could look at the sea
all day long; and to my students for their eagerness to
see this book finished. Many thanks also to everyone
at Search Press, especially Katie, who makes me
sound good! And to Debbie and Myk for their great
photography of my work.

Front cover
The Rhythm of the Sea
Original size 13 x 18cm (5 x 7in)
See page 41.

Page 1
The Pebbles Beneath
Original size 13 x 13cm (5 x 5in)
*A combination of the reflected sky and the rocks below the surface of the
water creates an intriguing mixture of colour in the foreground.*

Page 3
Surf's Up
Original size 13 x 13cm (5 x 5in)
*This headland is in the middle distance and therefore has more detail
and texture. It is completely covered in diagonal straight stitches with
highlights added in pale grey.*

Page 5
Running into the Sea
Original size 7.5 x 13cm (3 x 5in)
*A subtle change of colour from the foreground to the horizon, and a
transition from pale purple through cornflower blue to silvery blue and
green, reflect the calm nature of this piece and lead the eye along the
meandering stream into the sea.*

Mac ered s

Dedication

For Sue Smallwood.
A good friend sadly missed.

Contents

Introduction

A day on the beach means different things to us all. I tend to think of beaches as solitary places, particularly out of season when I am fully in tune with the weather and can experience its effects on the scenery: strong winds creating dramatic waves, the sound of seagulls, the light constantly changing as clouds move across the sky producing shade and revealing bright sunshine. When beaches are empty there is an immense feeling of distance, amplified by the sense of not knowing where the sea ends and the sky begins.

At a distance, a pebbled beach appears as small dots of colour in a familiar, subdued palette, but up close, beautiful combinations of browns, greys and bright oranges emerge. Colours are intense and vibrant when wet but disappointingly dull when dry. In rock pools, there is a depth of colour and an interesting play of reflections and textures under the surface of the water that is on the one hand fascinating, but also challenging to capture in machine embroidery.

I enjoy watching the hypnotic, ever-changing waves relentlessly tumbling on to the shoreline. I'm fascinated by the repetition of the shapes they create, how they develop, shifting in form and character as they swell and reach their full height to then dissipate in the shallows. Trying to capture them in stitch, in all their variations, is a constant challenge: as they roll, swell, foam, froth and then crash on to the rocks, exploding in sudden bursts of spray.

I have gathered ideas from all types of coastlines, from gentle waves lapping at sandy beaches to powerful surf rattling pebbles at my feet. The quality of light, time of day and location has a big influence on colour. The Mediterranean coast, for example, has a palette of bright turquoise-blue sea and warm ochre sand whereas North Atlantic coastlines in winter have a strong but limited palette of muted grey-green water, white waves and dark rocks. Both inspire me and I'm equally attracted to the different colour combinations.

I want my embroideries to capture the drama and atmosphere of the sea in order to convey a real sense of being there. I want you, the viewer, to imagine you can feel the wind and the warmth of the sun, and hear the clatter of waves breaking over pebbles. As with other subjects I have been attracted to and explored, I look for patterns, rhythms and colours, the sense of light and space and, most importantly, the textures. Then I find ways of expressing them in stitch.

This book is designed to encourage and inspire you to produce your own embroidered seascapes, and to discover, like me, the joy and satisfaction of expressing yourself artistically through freehand machine embroidery.

Across the Sea

Original size 15 x 30cm (6 x 12in)

This embroidery contains an interesting mix of ochres and blues. On the horizon, I used stripes of blues and turquoise executed in small stitches to create distance. The colours change in the middle distance to very dark browns and ochre, created by the shadows and reflections of the rocks. In the foreground, there is another range of tones as the transparency of the water reveals the shapes and colours of the stones beneath. Here I used long straight stitches to create a feeling of the water floating across the surface of the stones.

Materials & equipment

New products and equipment are always coming on to the market. My students are very good at introducing me to these but I have an established way of working and really the equipment I use hasn't changed much in 30 years. It has been a journey for me of experimenting and then settling on a range of materials and equipment that have become firm favourites.

Sewing equipment

Sewing machine

You can use any electric sewing machine to do freehand machine embroidery and it is possible to adapt a basic electric sewing machine very easily. You need to be able to remove the presser foot and lower the feed dog, which will allow you to move the embroidery in various directions and at any speed. You will be in control (with a little practice) of the length and direction of stitch. Remember, if you move the fabric slowly you will get small stitches and if you move it quickly you will get long stitches.

It is important that the machine is well maintained and oiled regularly for trouble-free sewing.

A machine set into a table is ideal for freehand machine embroidery, but otherwise an extension table attachment is a great substitute. This supports the embroidery hoop and allows you to slide the work smoothly under the needle for better control. A machine that has a swing needle and therefore does zigzag stitch as well as straight stitch will give you more variety of texture, and I prefer a dial or sliding lever to alter the width of zigzag stitch because it gives more flexibility than push-button controls.

Threads

You can use a wide variety of threads for machine embroidery – rayons and polyesters for example as long as they are good quality and colourfast. My personal preference is for pure cotton thread in a no. 50 weight. I like the fineness of this weight and the subtle sheen of the natural fibres.

I always buy threads in tonal ranges as these are more useful for the way I like to blend colours in my work. To increase the range of colours I can use I buy from several manufacturers. I keep my threads in open trays, in colour ranges – all the blues in one tray, for example, and all the greens in another – and find this makes selecting colours easier.

Silk

I use a white, medium-weight, 8mm habutai silk. I have tried many different fabrics for painting and embroidery and favour this because it paints beautifully, stretches taut in the frame, is strong and holds lots of stitches. It also has an even weave and natural sheen that complement the cotton threads I use.

For my paper and stitch embroideries I use a base of lightweight cotton or muslin.

Embroidery hoop

I recommend a 20cm (8in) wooden embroidery hoop with the inner hoop bound with fabric tape. The fabric stretched in the hoop needs to be flat and taut for the machine to stitch effectively without the fabric puckering, and a bound hoop grips the silk more successfully.

Machine bobbins

A selection of spare bobbins is useful because of the many colour changes needed. Always buy the correct ones for your machine and prepare a few before you start sewing, using the colours you know you will use.

Screwdrivers

A small screwdriver is needed to alter the tension screw on the bobbin, and a larger one to tighten the screw on the hoop.

Machine needles

I always use a size 80 (12) needle and make sure it's in good condition because a blunt needle will make pull lines in the silk.

Embroidery scissors

A sharp pair of embroidery scissors with pointed tips is essential for cutting threads close to the surface of the work.

The sewing equipment you need for making machine embroidered pictures.

Other equipment

Source photographs

Source photographs are essential; they are the inspiration and starting point of the embroidery.

Sketches

Sketches made either on location for recording composition ideas or detail, or at home as part of the planning process, help you bring ideas and elements together in one well-planned composition.

L-shaped cards

These help the design process by allowing you to crop sections of your source photographs.

Air/water-soluble pen

This is used to draw the basic design and details on the silk. It is air-soluble but can also be removed with water.

Resist

Resist is a clear gel used in a plastic pipette with a fine (0.3mm) nib. I use it to mark out the basic design on the silk. When dry, it stops the flow of the silk paints, helping to control where you put the background colours. When the dyes have been fixed the resist is washed out with hot, soapy water, leaving white lines in its place. It is sometimes called outliner or gutta.

Masking tape

I use this to tape the source photograph to the back of the silk if I am tracing the basic design with the air/water-soluble pen. I also use it to hold the L-shaped cards together and in place when cropping the photographs.

Ruler

Use a ruler to make sure the edges of the picture are straight and square. If you use the ruler to draw a line with resist, be careful not to smudge the wet line when moving the ruler away.

Tracing paper or acetate

If the basic design you wish to extract from the photograph is difficult to see through the silk, a tracing can be made on tracing paper or acetate as this will show more clearly through the silk.

Permanent marker

Use this to trace your design on to tracing paper or acetate using a strong, black line.

Silk frame

I use a simple, square wooden frame to stretch the silk on for painting. I secure the silk using three-pronged, metal pins.

Water pot

A container of water is needed for diluting the paint and cleaning your brushes when painting the background for your design.

Silk paints

Water-based silk paints are ideal for painting your background. They can be used straight from the bottle, diluted or mixed together to create a huge range of colours and tones. Simply add more water to make a paler shade.

Palette

I use a white, ceramic palette for mixing my paint colours – I can see the colours I am mixing clearly and it is easier to keep clean than a plastic palette.

Paintbrushes

I use watercolour brushes in a range of sizes from 000 to 8 for painting my backgrounds. The larger sizes are for washes of colour and the smaller sizes for detail.

Paper towel

Useful for removing excess paint or water from your brush, and for drying your brushes after washing them.

Inspiration

When I started to explore sea scenes, capturing the shape and movement of waves was my primary interest. I embarked on a fact-finding mission to the coast with my camera and sketchbook, and quickly discovered a wealth of imagery to inspire me.

These pages look like my studio desk, where I look through my photographs, pencil sketches and simple watercolour studies made on site. They are scattered around to give me ideas, creating the desire to embroider the places I have been to and recorded. It's a little chaotic but very inspiring, spurring me on to create in paint and stitch.

Sea scenes contain some of the most intriguing imagery to explore. The ever-shifting landscape is difficult to capture with the camera or in a sketch, and is even more challenging with a sewing needle. Attempting to recreate all the textures and shapes of a seascape in stitch is what drives me forwards to create new work. I feel that being stretched in this way is good for me as an artist – it forces me out of my comfort zone of familiar subjects and encourages me to explore new elements, colours and textures.

There is a wealth of variety in subject matter, from gentle waves lapping on a sandy Mediterranean beach to huge, dramatic waves crashing loudly on to rocks on a windswept coast; both create a very different atmosphere. But what all seascapes have in common is their repetitive nature. Pattern and rhythm are everywhere, from the rolling of white clouds across a blue sky to the movement of the waves. It is like watching a recording over and over again; wonderfully mesmerising and, for me, truly captivating.

Rocks and pebbles

Foreground rocks are wonderful for creating interest, especially when wet and glistening in the sunlight, which heightens their colour. Waves breaking over rocks create foam or spray, and patterns form as the water trickles down the rocks creating contrasting stripes of colour, texture and movement.

Sand

Dry sand has a totally different feel and colour palette to wet sand and it can add another layer to the foreground of a picture. As the sea recedes it leaves wet sand and puddles in which the sky is reflected, creating stripes of blue cutting across brown, ridged sand.

The textures and colours in pebbles and sand and the fascinating way the water moves and flows around and over them, eventually sinking or receding without trace, is great for foreground texture and interest.

Sand dunes and their long grasses evoke a sense of calm and shelter, triggering childhood memories of lying amongst them to keep out of the wind. They bring a different range of colours and fine linear texture into a seascape.

13

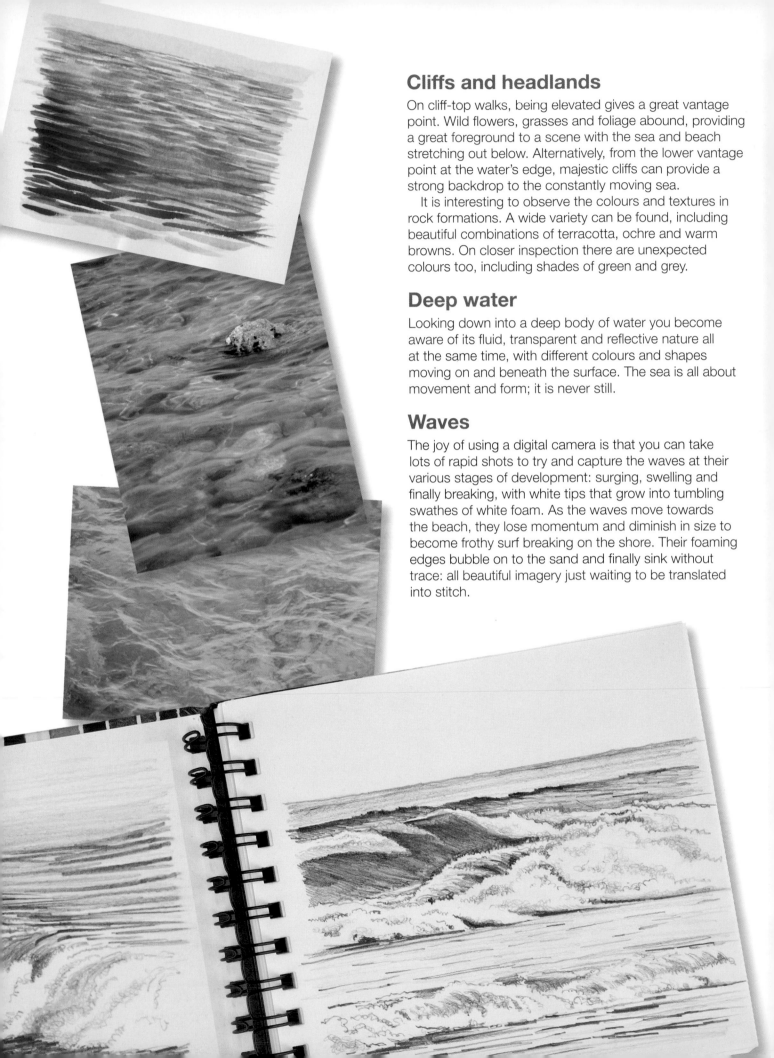

Cliffs and headlands

On cliff-top walks, being elevated gives a great vantage point. Wild flowers, grasses and foliage abound, providing a great foreground to a scene with the sea and beach stretching out below. Alternatively, from the lower vantage point at the water's edge, majestic cliffs can provide a strong backdrop to the constantly moving sea.

It is interesting to observe the colours and textures in rock formations. A wide variety can be found, including beautiful combinations of terracotta, ochre and warm browns. On closer inspection there are unexpected colours too, including shades of green and grey.

Deep water

Looking down into a deep body of water you become aware of its fluid, transparent and reflective nature all at the same time, with different colours and shapes moving on and beneath the surface. The sea is all about movement and form; it is never still.

Waves

The joy of using a digital camera is that you can take lots of rapid shots to try and capture the waves at their various stages of development: surging, swelling and finally breaking, with white tips that grow into tumbling swathes of white foam. As the waves move towards the beach, they lose momentum and diminish in size to become frothy surf breaking on the shore. Their foaming edges bubble on to the sand and finally sink without trace: all beautiful imagery just waiting to be translated into stitch.

Across the Bay

Original size 13 x 13cm (5 x 5in)

The viewpoint from high up on a cliff edge is wonderful. It is an opportunity to see the sea stretch out for miles to the horizon. The rocks punctuate the water and create shadows and reflections that give interesting colour changes to the water. The texture of the cliffs provides contrast and interest, and there is foreground detail in the form of foliage at your feet.

I always take lots of photographs and sometimes sketch on site to capture the main elements of the composition. It acts as a visual reminder of my intentions at the time.

Light and atmosphere

Every walk along a coastline or beach has a different atmosphere, depending on the location, time of day and season. The sense of light, tonal range and colours vary enormously depending on where you are in the world. The limited colour palette of a Northern European sea scene during the winter has a stark, cold, almost brutal feel to it. Dark shadows are created between white waves as they crash on to dark, forbidding rocks. The strong, contrasting colours of stormy seas create drama and excitement.

Alternatively, the warm tones of sunlit, ochre-coloured rocks and the deep-blue waters of the Mediterranean create a scene that conveys the heat of the day. Sparkling sunlight dances on the surface of the water and creates strongly contrasting deep blues and bright whites: with the gentle movement of the waves, the effect is hypnotic.

Rising Up From the Sea (above)

Original size 13 x 13cm (5 x 5in)

Interesting colour combinations are created by the reflections of the rocks in the foreground. There is a subtle merging of the sea and rocks and a sense of gentle movement in the waters of this sheltered bay.

The Rolling Surf (left)

Original size 13 x 18cm (5 x 7in)

Northern European seascapes have a unique palette. The sense of light is more subdued but just as beautiful as anywhere else.

I am fascinated by the transition of colour from the shoreline to the horizon: as you stand on a beach, notice how the pale hues in dry sand change subtly to the warm browns of wet sand showing through shallow waves. These then blend into pale blue as the water becomes deeper, moving then into increasingly strong blues, greens and turquoises. Within a certain depth of water, the sunlight bounces off the surface disguising abstract shapes of rocks underneath.

Sparkling Water

Original size 13 x 13cm (5 x 5in)

Intense greens, blues and turquoises on the shoreline fading to more subtle tones in the distance coupled with the terracotta-coloured rocks make the waters of the Channel Islands inspiring. The light here is very special: dancing across the surface of the water, it gives a shimmering palette of colour not found elsewhere.

18

Sunsets and sunrises are the most richly coloured embroideries in my seascapes range. The dramatic colour combinations and cloud formations reflected in the water have huge impact. I use a range of strong, bright yellows, oranges, reds and purples and incorporate interesting, abstract shapes in the clouds to add more texture and interest to this inspiring subject.

The Morning Sky

Original size 13 x 13cm (5 x 5in)

Sometimes I am inspired by scenes that are many miles apart. I wanted to combine the gentle sweep of the shoreline in the half light with a more interesting sky than the one that was there at the time. I found just what I wanted a few days later looking through my pantry window!

Composition

I always aim to design a balanced composition, incorporating certain elements in the scene: most important is a focal point, which could be the strong, curved shape of a breaking wave. I try to include areas of contrast too, such as white spray against black rocks; also, a sense of depth and perspective. This can be created by observing colour changes, from strong, contrasting foreground colours to muted shades towards the horizon; this is aerial perspective and is a subtle way of creating a sense of distance. Elements in the scene that are repeated will give perspective too, for example waves diminishing into the distance or the posts in a breakwater lead the eye into the picture and add to the sense of depth. This is linear perspective, and is a more obvious way to lead the eye into the picture. I also consider the use of light and shade, pattern, rhythm, colour and texture; all these elements hold an image together and make it a strong design.

The Breakwater

Original size 13 x 18cm (5 x 7in)

For the embroidery above it was difficult to get all the elements in the viewfinder of the camera at the same time: I wanted to combine the pebbles and puddles in the foreground, the angle of the breakwater and the view of the sea in the final composition. The solution was to take various detail shots for colour and reference and make a sketch of the overall scene. These are shown on the facing page. This method has worked for me many times, in this case giving me all the elements I want to feature in the composition, including foreground interest and a sense of depth and perspective created by the breakwater leading the eye into the scene.

Using sketches and photographs

Visiting a beach or stretch of coastline with an idea for an embroidery is always interesting. Capturing all the elements I want in a composition is sometimes difficult. The combination of finding the tide out and the constant movement of the sea brings a new set of challenges to composing a picture, so I take lots of photographs for colour and detail reference and a sketch or photograph of the overall scene.

Of course, the sea is constantly moving and some wave shapes are more interesting than others. I find a viewpoint that gives a good composition and take as many shots as I can so that the waves are captured at their various stages and the best shapes can be combined in embroidery.

I break away from the fixed proportions that the camera gives by cropping a photograph either with two L-shaped pieces of card over a print or on the computer. It changes the balance of the composition; cropping out a section of the sea, for example, will emphasise a dramatic sky. Another way is by joining two or more photographs together to create a wide vista or long, vertical view of the beach, sea and sky.

When I am back in my studio I gather together all the sketches and photographs that relate to a particular scene. I decide on all the elements I want to incorporate and on the overall dimensions and make a simple sketch plan of the composition. This, in conjunction with the source photographs and sketches, is what I need to move on to the next stage.

Perspective

A sense of depth and perspective in a piece can be achieved in several ways. One effective method is through observing colour changes, from strong contrasting foreground colours to muted shades towards the horizon. The scale and quantity of the stitches used also help give a sense of perspective. Small stitches or painted detail on the horizon pushes it into the distance, whereas in the foreground I build up texture by stitching on the spot and also by using long stitches, which make the foreground more prominent.

Planning the order of work is crucial to create perspective. Typically you would work from distance to foreground so that the elements physically overlap each other, adding to the illusion of depth. This is explained more fully in the projects on pages 62–94.

Frothy Waves

Original size 10 x 18cm (4 x 7in)

The colours in this embroidery are based on colour sketches made at the time. The photographs (shown on the left) were disappointingly dull so I injected the colour back in with threads and paint. Also, selecting the best waves from a series of photographs I took at the time enabled me to incorporate all the shapes I wanted. Lengthening the image made space for sky and headland at the top and pebbles on the beach below, so the fixed proportions of the camera didn't dictate my final composition.

Planning an embroidery

When planning an embroidery there are many decisions to be made. With the sketches and source photographs to analyse, I look carefully at achieving a range of different interpretations within the composition. I look at the overall dimensions, colour and content and how I want to portray each area.

I always use a mixture of silk painting and stitch, working some heavily stitched areas for greater texture and some painted areas to give detail that looks more distant or contrasts well with the stitching. Other areas are lightly stitched to let the paint show through.

Design

When I am ready to start designing an embroidery, I gather together all the sketches and photographs I have that relate to a particular scene. I decide on all the elements I want to incorporate in the embroidery and on the overall dimensions, then make a simple sketch plan of the composition, in which I simplify the picture and break it down into distinct sections. This helps me to organise the shapes and colours needed for the painted background. It also provides useful guidelines to work within at the embroidery stage.

Paint or stitch?

More textured areas, such as rough seas and windblown grasses, lend themselves to stitch, whereas smooth areas, such as distant sea and sky, are better represented by silk painting. All areas are painted at the start of a project, the detailed painting sitting alongside the simple silk-paint washes that are needed as a base for the embroidered areas.

Choosing colours

I look at the colours in the photographs and sketches and match my threads and paint to them, but occasionally the memories I have of being on the beach and being inspired by the scene before me suggest a greater intensity of colour than my watercolours or photographs show. Having the freedom to change the colour of the paint and the threads you use will enable you to recreate your memory of the scene more accurately. Remember, your photographs and sketches provide a record of the scene that inspired you, and there is always the potential to move forwards from that point to create something even more evocative of the moment.

This partly worked version of 'Beyond the Breakwater' shows clearly how the smooth, painted areas contrast with the more textured stitching. For areas that I intend to stitch, a simple wash of colour is sufficient as a base. These include the waves, which have a simple wash of blue paint, and the breakwater, which has a wash of dark brown. The sky and water on the horizon are interpreted in paint and are left unstitched, and here more detail has been painted on to the silk. This creates a softer, more distant effect against which the stitched foaming waves below stand out, adding to the sense of depth and perspective. In the foreground, the smooth reflections in the shallow water have also been painted.

Beyond the Breakwater

Original size 13 x 13cm (5 x 5in)

On completion of the stitched areas of this picture, I assessed the balance and tonal range of the composition. I decided it needed more detail and strength in the painted foreground, so I darkened the painted reflections so they linked in with the strong colour and texture of the stitched breakwater. I also added some small, horizontal dots of colour to suggest a little texture in the sand showing through the shallow water.

Painting a background

Once you have decided upon the composition size, content and how you intend to interpret the various elements in paint or stitch, you then need to decide how each area of the composition should be painted. For areas that will have stitched detail, a simple wash of colour is sufficient. This means that it doesn't have to be stitched too heavily and any small areas of silk that do show through will blend in with the stitches. For areas of painted detail, a lot more time and attention is needed at this stage.

This is an example of a source photograph and the painted background derived from it ready to be stitched. Having transferred the image to the silk (see page 28), I decided to create perspective by leaving the mountains and sky as painted areas. These were therefore painted freehand, without the use of resist, as I didn't want a white line outlining the tops of the mountains. The sky was painted first because it is paler then, when dry, I carefully painted both mountains with a small brush in a mid grey. When these were dry I used a smaller brush to paint a series of diagonal lines in a darker grey over the mountain on the right-hand side to give it some detail and definition. I have kept the painting of the sea simplistic, just marking the positions of the white water and rocks in resist as guidelines for the stitching stage.

I have changed the colours a little from the photograph, using a richer green tone for the water and making the sky paler so that the shapes of the mountains are more clearly defined. I also noticed that the sea was darker on the right-hand side so I have painted it accordingly. I have painted the appropriate colour in each area knowing my thread colours will blend in with the paint.

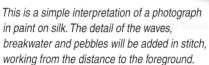

This is a simple interpretation of a photograph in paint on silk. The detail of the waves, breakwater and pebbles will be added in stitch, working from the distance to the foreground.

In the Dunes

Original size 6.5 x 10cm (2½ x 4in)

A sketch of the grasses blowing in the wind with the tide out and a great sense of space was all the inspiration I needed for this embroidery. With the help of some photographs for colour reference, I painted the background (shown on the left) freehand and stitched just the sea nearest the shore and the foreground grasses.

Transferring a design

Before you can paint, you need to transfer your design to the silk. Begin by stretching white, medium-weight, 8mm habutai silk on to a square wooden frame. Use silk pins to anchor it down and keep it flat and taut.

Draw on the basic design with an air/water-soluble pen, either freehand or by tracing your photograph or sketch through the silk. When you are happy with it, draw over the lines with resist. Once this is dry it will act as a barrier between adjacent coloured areas, controlling the spread of the paint. There will be a white line wherever you have put resist, so make the line wide enough to hold your paint but thin enough not to compromise the design.

If you want painted areas of different colours side by side without a white line in between, paint the paler of the two colours first and let it dry then overlap the edge with the darker shade. When painting on an area of dry paint, the wet paint doesn't spread as much as it does on unpainted silk, so this becomes another method of controlling the paint.

As a general rule, use a small brush for smaller areas and a larger brush for larger areas, and paint within the lines of resist. The paint will spread and blend easily on the silk, so work slowly using gentle, horizontal brushstrokes.

Keep the sky simple so that all the emphasis is on the sea. In the design below, the sky is the most important part of the painting process, as it won't be stitched on.

Note

The step-by-step demonstration below provides the painted background for the project on pages 62–73. The photographs and sketch that inspired it are provided on page 62.

1 Place your sketch on a raised surface underneath the silk so that it is just touching the surface and draw over the lines using an air/water-soluble pen. Draw it freehand, if you prefer. Put in the frame and the main elements of the design only. Make sure the design is divided into distinct sections, as defined by the background colour or type of stitching you intend to use.

2 When you are happy with your design, go over the lines with resist applied using a fine-nib pen. Draw with a continuous line, and go round the outline too. The line of resist between the sea and the sky is particularly important otherwise colour will seep from one to the other. Allow to dry thoroughly.

3 Make two tones of blue silk paint – one light blue and one slightly darker. Test them on the edge of the silk to make sure they are the right colour. Paint the sky, starting with the lighter blue at the bottom and then the darker blue at the top, using horizontal brushstrokes. Leave a narrow gap between the two bands of colour to resemble a wispy cloud.

4 Mix black and brown paint together to make a dark brown base for the rocks. Paint on the colour, keeping within the lines.

5 For the sea, mix blue and green paint and add a little brown if necessary for a more subdued colour. Test the colour on the side of the silk, as before. When you are happy with it, paint the sea down to the foreground section, again keeping within the line.

Tip

Avoid painting right up to the lines of resist; instead allow the paint to flow from the brush and spread up to the lines naturally.

6 Water down the blue-green mix and paint the foreground section of the sea.

7 Finally, mix a watery grey-brown for the beach and paint this on to complete the painted background.

8 The completed background. When the painting is dry, it is fixed to keep it colourfast by ironing with a hot iron for three minutes. It is then washed in hot, soapy water to remove the resist, rinsed and then ironed dry.

Starting to stitch

I view this stage of the creative process as playing with textured mark making. Finding a technique in stitch to replicate certain textures within the sea and its adjoining imagery is very exciting. I use only two simple machine stitches – straight stitch and zigzag stitch – and vary the length and shape of the stitch with the speed and direction of the hoop. By then making subtle changes to the thread colour in the bobbin and on the top of the machine, I can produce a myriad of painterly effects.

Setting up the machine

Getting your machine ready for freehand machine embroidery is easy – simply remove the presser foot and lower the feed dog. These changes allow you to move the embroidery hoop in any direction and at any speed, so you are in control of the length and direction of the stitches. If you move the hoop slowly you will get small stitches and if you move it quickly you will get longer stitches.

Stitch tension

Altering the thread tension on the sewing machine will add to the different effects you can create in order to build texture and blend colours. I always try to pull up the bobbin thread to appear on the surface of the embroidery by tightening the top tension, and if this doesn't work I loosen the bobbin tension as well. The top tension is tightened by moving the tension dial or buttons to a higher number or towards the + sign. The bobbin thread tension is loosened by turning the small screw on the bobbin case anticlockwise. If you are nervous of doing this, you can buy a spare bobbin case and use it for freehand machine embroidery only. Experiment with a variety of tensions on the top of the machine and in the bobbin to see the different effects you can achieve.

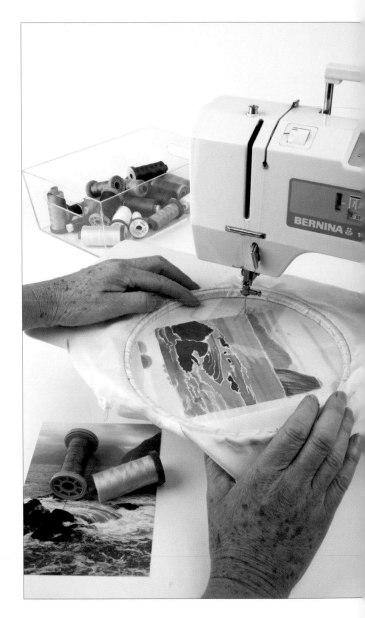

Tip

A good way of remembering by how much you have altered your bobbin thread tension is to think of the screw as a clock face and count the number of 'minutes' you have moved it, for example '15 minutes clockwise' or '30 minutes anticlockwise'. It is then easy to put it back to where you started.

Using an embroidery hoop

Stretching the background painting in an embroidery hoop keeps the fabric taut and square. Make sure the painted design is facing upwards and the fabric lies level with the lower edge of the hoop (this is to ensure it lies flat against the surface of the machine as you stitch). If your design is larger than the hoop, make sure the part you want to stitch first is within the frame; you can move the hoop later as your embroidery progresses. Manipulate the fabric to make sure it is pulled evenly and tightly all the way round the hoop, and check that the horizon is completely straight.

Use a 20cm (8in) bound hoop. By binding the inner hoop with cotton tape you will be able to obtain a better grip on the fabric and stretch it really tightly in the hoop. This is important as it prevents the fabric from puckering and the machine will stitch properly. If the machine misses stitches or breaks a thread or a needle, this may be because the fabric is not taut enough in the hoop.

When you are ready to stitch, place the hoop and fabric under the machine, and pull up the bobbin thread and lower the presser foot before you start.

To have the best control of the hoop, rest your forearm or elbow on the table and make sure the movements you make are with your fingers, not with your arms. Try to keep your shoulders relaxed and make sure your chair is the right height for the table and machine.

Choosing threads

By matching threads to my photographs and colour sketches, I put together the range I intend to use. For the best match I always do this in good, natural light. I start by choosing one colour within an area and then add lighter and darker shades of that colour until I have the full tonal range I need. I find holding the whole reel of cotton over the photograph works well rather than just looking at a single thread. I then move from area to area within the photograph or sketch, repeating the process until I have colours selected for the whole picture. It can be useful at this stage to make notes about what colour goes where on a simple pencil sketch of the design.

As the work progresses, I often add an extra colour or two. It isn't always obvious until the colours are worked together that a lighter or darker tone needs to be added to the range.

Identifying the proportion of each colour within an area is important. Having selected the shades of blue within a wave, for example, the next stage is to decide how much of each colour to use, for example 10 per cent dark blue, 70 per cent mid blue and 20 per cent light blue.

Tip

If stretching the fabric doesn't straighten the horizon, turn the hoop over and place a ruler along the horizon. Draw a line using an air/water-soluble pen. The ink will show on the right side of the work and provide a straight line to stitch along.

Stitching

Having identified which colours you need and in what quantities to use them, the next decision is about the shapes of the various elements that make up the picture. You need to train your eye to notice the shapes formed. These can be quite abstract and can be more easily identified by turning the source photograph upside down. This lets you see the shapes clearly because you are no longer interpreting them as familiar objects. The drawn guidelines on your silk background will help you to place your stitches correctly.

Using just straight stitch and zigzag stitch, you can use your sewing machine like a paintbrush to produce thin lines (straight stitch) and broad lines (zigzag stitch). Don't be afraid to experiment – move the hoop in different ways and notice the effects it creates.

Straight stitch

With the machine set on straight stitch, move the hoop slowly to produce small stitches; quickly to make long stitches; diagonally in straight lines and curved lines; and in short jagged or spiralling movements to create many different effects.

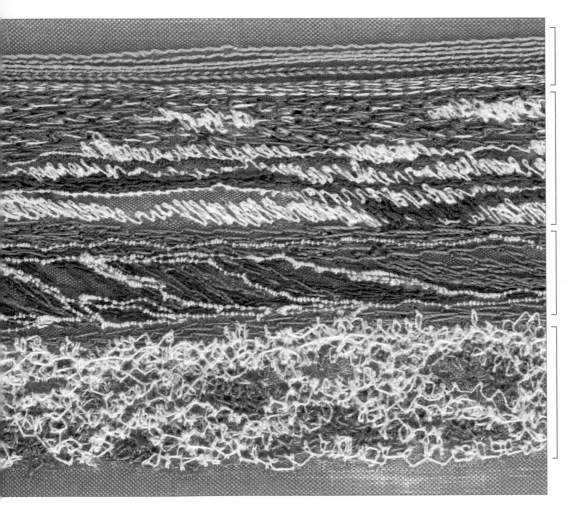

Practise parallel, straight lines; it's easier to move the hoop backwards and forwards than from side to side so turn the hoop 90˚. Move the hoop slowly for small stitches and more quickly for a long stitch.

Small, jagged movements of the hoop will produce more textured effects. Try moving the hoop in a diagonal direction and horizontally. Keep the movement of your fingers compact to create small-scale marks. This type of effect is good for working distant areas.

Try meandering lines following the curves and contours of a shape. Tighten the top tension to pull up a white thread from the bobbin for a broken line of colour.

Spiralling movements of the hoop, with the same colour in the bobbin as in the top of the machine, produce a different type of effect. Soft, rounded shapes can overlap each other and build up texture.

Play around with the colour combinations threaded on to the machine and make sure the top tension is tightened enough to pull the bobbin thread to the surface.

Zigzag stitch

With the machine set on zigzag, how you move the hoop will affect the marks it will make. Try, for example, moving the hoop slowly and then quickly from side to side. You can also hold the hoop on the spot and let the stitches build up on top of each other, and alter the stitch width for a change of scale. Vary the angle of the hoop under the machine so that the zigzag stitches lie in different directions on the silk.

Using darker tones in the bobbin than on the top of the machine creates a shadow and makes the texture you create look more three dimensional.

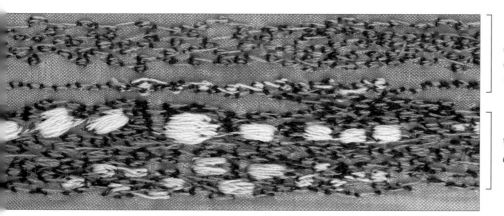

With the machine set on a narrow width of zigzag, move the hoop horizontally, on the spot, from one set of stitches to the next.

Vary the size of the zigzag and the colours, and mix them together.

This is a small zigzag with a dark grey bobbin thread. Leave spaces for another colour to be added.

Work with a large zigzag. Let it build up on the spot for more texture.

Vary the angle of the hoop and move the hoop to make some larger shapes.

33

Elements of seascapes

Seascapes are full of intriguing abstract shapes, and there is a skill in analysing what size, colour and direction of stitch to use to portray them. Making decisions about the order of work within each section can be difficult at first, though generally I would recommend working from dark tones through to highlights. Consider the length and quantity of stitches used as this will have an impact on the finished result.

Water

To create a sense of perspective, small running stitches are used in the distance and larger running and zigzag stitches in the foreground. More texture can be created by overlapping the stitches and working them on top of each other. Work from the distance to the foreground and from dark tones to light tones within each section of your design.

Distant water

Horizontal, parallel lines of closely worked small straight stitches are used to give the impression of distant water. The area from the horizon forward to the middle distance may have no visible waves or other elements, such as rocks, that break it up and give a sense of perspective. The size of the stitch used therefore becomes very important. Work very small stitches on the horizon and gradually increase their length as you move forwards. This change in scale of the stitches combined with thin, horizontal stripes of different colours will create an impression of distance and perspective. The subtle changes of colour in this area are sometimes difficult to identify, but turning your source photograph upside down can help you to see them.

It requires a bit of practice to stitch straight lines freehand. Some people find it easier to stitch a straight line by moving the hoop up and down rather than from side to side, so try turning your embroidery through 90°.

To achieve a flat, straight, horizontal line of stitching for the sea, start approximately 2mm (1/8in) down from the horizon. That will allow you a couple of wobbly lines while you get into the rhythm of moving the hoop slowly backwards and forwards. If the painted horizon wasn't quite straight or horizontal when you secured the silk in the hoop, this is an opportunity to correct it.

Rise and Fall

Original size 15 x 20.5cm (6 x 8in)

The gentle movement of the waves creates interesting patterns in foam which float on the surface of the water.

It is easier to control the hoop and create straight lines over a short distance, so if the horizon is wide it is better to stitch across it in sections. Feather the sections together with irregular edges so that they don't appear as distinct blocks, and finish by stitching a few horizontal lines across the whole area to link the sections together.

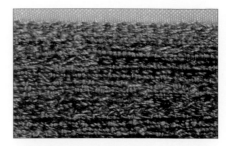

Distant water (see page 34).

Choppy water

Moving forwards from the horizon to where the sea has more movement, use a more textured stitch with a contrasting bobbin colour. Straight stitches worked horizontally moving three stitches forwards then one stitch back are a good way to create texture. To make the bobbin colour more visible, pull it to the surface by tightening the top tension. This will create a fragmented effect if the top colour is very different from the bobbin colour, or a strong line if the top and bobbin colours are the same.

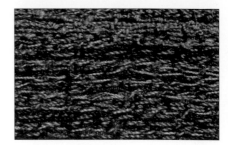

Choppy water (see left).

Distant breaking waves

As waves break in the distance, the typical 'white horses' imagery comes to mind. The tapered white edge is the most distinctive feature of these waves, so it is important to replicate it as accurately as possible. Because these waves are in the distance you are working at a small scale, so aim to capture an impression of the overall shape rather than a detailed interpretation. Use small, diagonal, jagged straight stitches in increasing and decreasing length with white on top of the machine as well as in the bobbin.

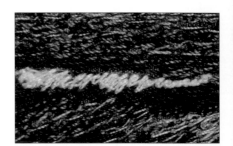

Breaking wave (see left).

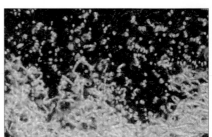

Speckles of spray (see page 40).

Enlarged sections of the embroidery shown on the facing page.

A gentle swell

Identify the shapes within the wave that give it perspective and, if necessary, exaggerate those shapes or apply more of them to emphasise the effect they create. There is often a subtle blending of colours needed to mimic the gentle rise and fall of the water, so shades that show a gradual change in tone from light to dark work well. Use curved lines of straight stitch closely worked following the shape of the wave.

Crashing Through Rocks

Original size 13 x 18cm (5 x 7in)

There are many elements within this embroidery. The calm, dark blue water beyond the rocks contrasts well with the melee of milky white foam and spray in the foreground.

Foaming waves

Foaming waves are rounded, tumbling shapes best interpreted using small spirals of straight stitch in a range of tones, darkest first, to create depth. For more texture, overlap the stitches. Look for the shapes of the shadows in the white waves to give depth and form to the foam. These pale blue or grey shadows will need to be stitched first.

Breaking Waves

Original size 18 x 13cm (7 x 5in)

The strong silhouette of the rock makes a bold backdrop for the movement in the waves as they tumble and then dissipate on the sand.

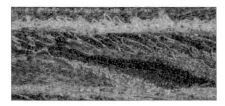

A gentle swell (see page 36).

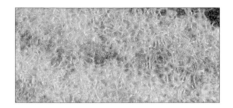

Foaming waves (see page 38).

Enlarged sections of the embroidery shown on the left.

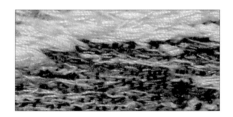

Waves breaking on the beach (see page 40).

Foreground pebbles (see page 43).

Enlarged sections of the embroidery shown on the right.

The Rolling Waves

Original size 10 x 18cm (4 x 7in)

The repetition of the foam constantly arriving at the water's edge and sinking into the pebbles is hypnotic.

Calm dappled water

In the middle distance or foreground, within a colourful body of water, there are often small areas of isolated or fragmented colour (see 'Rising Up From the Sea' on page 17). These are created by movement and the reflection of light. The best approach to interpreting this effect is to identify the predominant colour and then stitch all the small sections of fragmented colour first (there may be several of these). Finally, work the predominant colour around and through these smaller sections. This will cover up any connecting stitch lines, blend the colours and give a more cohesive feel generally to this area of your embroidery. This technique can be executed with straight stitch or a wide zigzag worked horizontally.

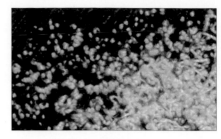

Speckles of spray (see left).

Speckles of spray

Sections of spray are disconnected from the bulk of a wave and will show up against dark rocks or distant water as separate dots of white. This can be difficult to interpret in stitch. It is achieved by using straight stitch, and having a loose bobbin tension. Put white thread in the bobbin and the colour of the rocks or water on the top of the machine, then pull up a small loop of the bobbin to the surface. The top thread will blend into the background and only the white stitches will show as separate flecks.

Floating foam (see left).

Enlarged sections of the embroidery shown on the right.

Floating foam

To create the impression of floating foam found in the flat areas between waves, lay down a foundation of horizontal straight stitches in dark and mid tones and then use drifts of horizontal zigzag stitches in white for the foam. A long stitch length is very important as is a loose bobbin tension so that the top thread floats across the surface.

Waves breaking on the beach

The leading edge of the wave on the shoreline is textured. Various widths of zigzag worked horizontally in drifts and on the spot are a good way to interpret this.

The Rhythm of the Sea

Original size 13 x 18cm (5 x 7in)

This embroidery incorporates a lot of the elements of the sea that I find fascinating. A variety of waves that swell, froth, foam and crash against the rocks, creating pattern, texture and rhythm.

Pebbles

The colour and appearance of pebbles varies with distance, so capturing these changes as you move from the background to the foreground of a picture will introduce perspective to your embroidery. In the distance, the colours are more muted and blended, whereas towards the foreground the colours are stronger in tone and contrast and the variety of colours becomes more obvious. To create perspective, use small stitches in the distance and increase the size and quantity of stitches as you progress forwards to the foreground. Use a darker tone in the bobbin than on the top of the machine to help create depth.

The embroidery below shows the stitches used to create different effects as you move towards the foreground. Each of these effects is described in more detail in the following pages.

A Walk on the Beach

Original size 10 x 18cm (4 x 7in)

Building up texture with a wide zigzag stitch is the perfect way to interpret the texture of the foaming waves and the pebble beach.

Distant pebbles.

Middle-distance pebbles.

Foreground pebbles.

Enlarged sections of the embroidery shown on the left.

Distant pebbles

Use a small straight stitch in parallel, horizontal lines in various colours worked closely together.

Middle-distance pebbles

Use straight stitches in a range of tones worked horizontally to create this effect. Moving the hoop backwards and forwards, for example three stitches forwards and one stitch back, will create texture and a slightly larger scale. Rows of horizontal spiralling straight stitch can also look very effective.

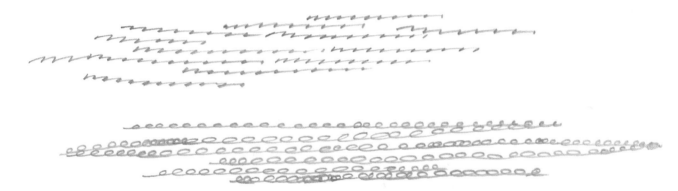

Foreground pebbles

In the foreground, the extensive range of colours is more apparent, and it is possible to distinguish individual pebbles and stones. The colours need to be applied one at a time and in a range of sizes to suggest variety. For each colour, move horizontally from pebble to pebble as much as possible so that the connecting threads blend in, and leave spaces in between that can be filled in with different colours later to obtain a random effect. You can vary the size of a pebble by altering the amount of stitching on it, so hold the hoop still for longer on some pebbles than others. Extra texture and depth can be created by working zigzag stitches on the spot. Alter the angle of the hoop a little so that the zigzags are not all horizontal. This makes the foreground look more natural.

If there is a discernible shadow to a single pebble, this can be painted on to the silk afterwards or stitched before the pebble so that it appears to lie underneath.

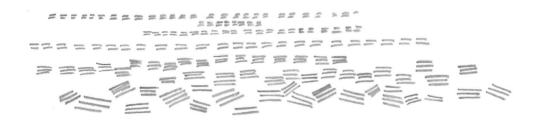

Rocks

A wide zigzag will work for small rocks in the foreground (see page 33). Move the hoop a little sideways to form a larger block of stitches and tilt the picture 45° to angle the zigzag and add variety.

For more detail in foreground rocks, parallel rows of straight stitch work best (see page 32). These will allow the rocks to be represented in more detail, either with graduated colour on smooth surfaces or more texture on rough surfaces.

Relentless Waves

Original size 18 x 13cm (7 x 5in)

Hypnotic waves crashing into stark, jagged rocks produced this image, which is full of contrast and movement.

Cliffs and headlands

For cliffs, following the strata of the rocks with a straight stitch is the best approach. Observe the direction of the subtle stripes of colour: it could be horizontal, vertical or diagonal. Observing and recreating the shadows and highlights is important.

To create distant headlands use paint in soft, muted tones. If there is more detail, texture and strength needed to make them more prominent then add some stitches. If it is difficult to analyse the direction of stitch to use, small, diagonal running stitches will always work well.

The View from Here

Original size 10 x 15cm (4 x 6in)

A series of horizontal and vertical straight stitches was used for the cliffs on the left-hand side of the picture, starting with the dark shadows and moving on to the mid tones. Highlights were then added, blending the colours together with small stitches.

A Gentle Swell

Original size 13 x 13cm (5 x 5in)

In any sea scene there are strong, intense colours and tonal contrast in the foreground and softer, more muted gradations of colour in the distance. This is what gives the picture aerial perspective. There can be an almost seamless join between sky and sea; a subtle change from green to blue at an indiscernible point, adding to the sense of space and distance.

A Rocky Shore

Original size 7.5 x 13cm (3 x 5in)

The foreground rocks are worked in diagonal lines of straight stitch to suggest the strata of the rock. These contrast well with the horizontal lines of stitching for the sky.

Frothy Waves

Original size 10 x 18cm (4 x 7in)

The wide variety of stitch techniques used within each wave adds to the sense of movement in this piece.

Cliff Top Walk

Original size 35.5 x 23cm (14 x 9in)

A breezy walk along the headland was very inspiring, with the colour of the heather, the texture of the exposed rocks and the movement of the tall grasses. I took many photographs and composed this picture to try and capture the sense of space, which was the overriding sensation at the time.

Skies

When drawing inspiration from the sea, it is natural to include the sky as part of the picture, usually as a secondary feature. During sunrise and sunset the sky is more dramatic due to the shapes and colours in the cloud formations, and it can become the focal point.

The sky can be interpreted completely in stitch or in a combination of painted silk and stitch. The method you choose depends upon the amount of texture to be found in the scene.

Along the Coast

Original size 7.5 x 13cm (3 x 5in)

The sky and sea are stitched in horizontal straight stitches with the smallest stitches used for the horizon. To create perspective, these stitches increase in size towards the top of the sky and the bottom of the sea. The foreground rocks are simply stitched in dark brown in a diagonal direction to contrast with the other areas.

Shepherd's Warning

Original size 13 x 13cm (5 x 5in)

The sky at the coast seems to go on for ever and, at sunset, with glorious colours reflected in the sea, it is an inspiration. Depicting the sea and sky where they share the same colours but vary in scale and texture is a fascinating challenge. The sea looks smooth and calm and the clouds appear strangely solid in their form. To give texture, the sky, water and rocks are all stitched.

Along the Beach

Original size 13 x 13cm (5 x 5in)

This sky is a combination of painted and stitched areas. The blue area is painted and looks smooth and distant. It lets the texture of the stitched clouds come forward, giving depth to the work. The clouds are worked in zigzag stitch, moving the hoop slowly to let the stitches build up on top of each other. Small straight stitches on the horizon and large zigzag stitches at the top of the sky add to the sense of perspective achieved.

If you decide to interpret the whole sky in stitch, it is still a good idea to have a painted background. It provides a base of colours and shapes that act as guidelines and you don't have to stitch so heavily when the correct colour is beneath the stitches. It doesn't need to be a complex painting as the detail will be executed in stitch.

The other approach is to use a combination of painted and stitched areas side by side. Paint can be used to represent an area within the sky that is less textured, for example on the horizon or in between cloud formations.

Project: Sunset

The design for this project was painted freehand with the intention of stitching only the clouds, the sea and the headland. The distant headland and the upper area of the sky are to remain unstitched.

You will need

Medium-weight white habutai silk

Wooden frame on which to stretch the silk

Silk pins

Air/water-soluble pen

Resist in a pipette with a nib

Silk paints and brushes

Water pot

Iron to fix the paints

Embroidery hoop

Sewing machine

Threads and bobbins (see opposite)

Embroidery scissors

Iron to fix the paints

1 Begin by outlining the various elements – the sun, clouds, distant mountains and headland – using air/water-soluble pen followed by resist (see page 28). Note that I have distinguished the main part of the headland that is in the foreground from the two points of land that extend into the sea in the mid-ground. I plan to use different colours for them all.

2 To paint the sky, make three mixes – dark orange, mid orange and yellow – in the palette and test the colours by placing a small brushstroke of each on the silk and letting them dry.

3 With a medium-sized brush, apply the mid orange very quickly in two horizontal lines at the top of the sky. With the dark orange, paint another two horizontal lines below it, close enough for the colours to merge. While still wet, lay streaks of yellow through the orange with a small brush. Rub over the surface gently with a dry finger to help blend the shades together.

4 For the sea, mix three different shades of brown and paint them on in the same way as you painted the sky, from pale to dark in horizontal lines.

Tip

It is important to work quickly so the paint doesn't dry before the next tone is applied, and the colours blend without a hard edge. This is more important if the area is to remain unstitched.

A selection of the threads and loaded bobbins that I used for this project. Be prepared to add in more colours as your embroidery progresses, and don't be afraid to change your mind if one or more of your initial choices simply doesn't work.

5 Finally, paint the headland using dark brown and black mixed together, and the distant mountains and clouds using a mix of brown and blue.

6 When the paint is dry, fix the paints then wash the silk (see page 29). Secure the silk in a 20cm (8in) bound hoop. You are now ready to start stitching.

7 With yellow on the top and in the bobbin, put in the highlights on the clouds using small straight stitches. Cover over the white lines left by the lines of resist.

Tip

To keep the stitch lines horizontal and straight, lay a ruler across the back of the silk while it is secured in the hoop, and draw in some straight lines using an air/ water-soluble pen to guide you. These will fade in time.

8 Change to orange thread on the top and in the bobbin and start to fill the area between the clouds and the tops of the mountains. Use horizontal lines of small straight stitches worked next to each other, with no gaps in between, but not overlapping. Leave some spaces just above the mountains (these will be filled with a different colour), and take some of the stitching across the sun and around the tops of the clouds, just beneath the yellow highlight.

9   Leave the same colour in the bobbin and put a slightly darker version on the top of the machine. Tighten the top tension to pull up the bobbin thread, then work into any gaps left in the previous stitching, just above the mountains, using the same stitch length and technique as before. Cover the white line left by the resist on the top of the mountain.

10   Place mid brown in the bobbin and a pink-brown on the top and work horizontal lines of very small straight stitches across the distant part of the sea, just below the mountains, covering the white line. As you come further forwards, space out the lines of stitching and gradually increase the stitch length to give perspective.

11   Put the pink-brown in the bobbin and light brown on top and work diagonal lines of straight stitching over the small point of land that is in the background. The diagonal lines will help distinguish the land from the sea.

12   With a warm dark brown on the top and very dark brown in the bobbin, work the larger of the two points of land using the same technique.

13   Put very dark grey on the top of the machine and black in the bobbin. Work the upper part of the headland using short, jagged, diagonal lines. Leave some gaps in the stitching so that the background colour shows through. Increase the length of stitch towards the base of the headland to give it perspective.

Sunset Sky

Original size 13 x 13cm (5 x 5in)

The completed embroidery. The remainder of the headland is worked using a warm dark brown on the top and black in the bobbin. Move the hoop in short, jagged movements and angle each line of stitching slightly differently to give the foreground texture and depth.

Paper & stitch

By experimenting with paper as a base for my embroidery I am actually revisiting a method of working from my days as a student. I used a collage of hand-dyed silk and incorporated paper as a base before I moved on to using painted silk backgrounds.

Tearing and layering different-coloured handmade papers to form a collage can be a looser, more flexible way of working than using a painted silk base. With its various textures and integrated fibres, very interesting effects can be achieved. Stitches are used to enhance the colour and texture of the paper. They can also be used to blend together the edges of the different-coloured paper pieces.

After the stitches are in place, a sharp pair of scissors or a large needle can be used to scratch away small pieces of paper, or alternatively small cuts can be made and parts of the top layer torn away to reveal the colours underneath. White paper layered underneath blue can be used to create the effect of rolling waves.

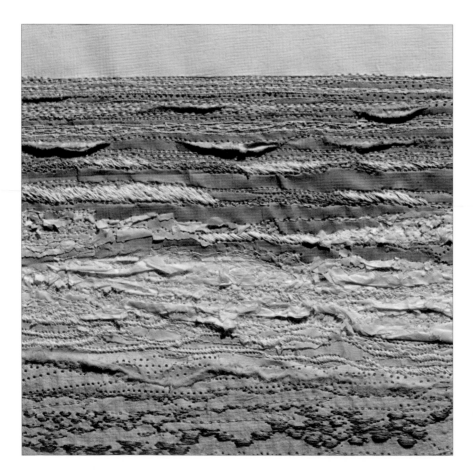

Breaking Waves

Original size 10 x 10cm (4 x 4in)

With a foundation of white paper underneath blue, I stitched a series of horizontal stitch lines and then made small horizontal cuts in the paper. Sections of the paper were peeled back to reveal the colours underneath, creating the effect of breaking waves. Various widths of zigzag stitch worked on the spot form the foreground pebbles.

Paper

You can use any type of paper for this technique, and experiment with cut and torn edges to achieve different effects. I favour handmade paper because it has some interesting textures, fibres and colours mixed into it. Tissue paper gives an interesting effect because it is semi-transparent. When layered, other colours will show through, making shading and blending possible. Tissue can also be crumpled, twisted into shapes and stitched down to give a highly textured feel. Ready-printed, torn-up paper bags can be effective too.

Experiment with layers of different colours. Choose the colours you use underneath carefully if you intend to scratch away some of the top layers to reveal them.

Rolling Waves

Original size 10 x 10cm (4 x 4in)

Textured, handmade paper torn, layered and stitched into, creates depth and a strong, three-dimensional quality to this scene.

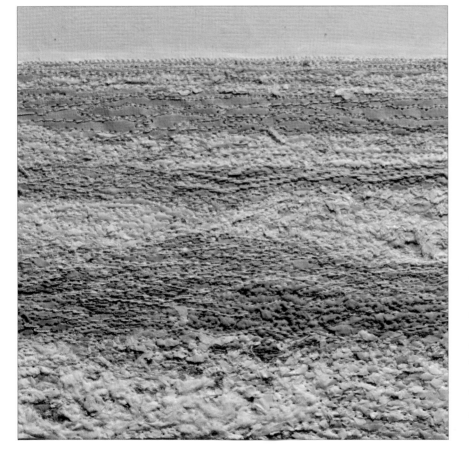

Foaming Waves

Original size 10 x 10cm (4 x 4in)

Here, only three different colours are used as the paper base for the sea and sky and these are stitched into place with horizontal straight stitches in a paler colour. The waves are created with crumpled layers of thin, white tissue paper stitched down with white thread and then sections are scratched away to reveal the blue and green paper underneath. The more layers of tissue there are, the more texture is created.

57

Project: Relentless Waves

As with my embroideries, I use photographs as a starting point for my paper and stitch projects, and create a basic layout that captures the background colours and proportions of the composition. In addition to the usual materials and equipment required for machine embroidery (see pages 8–11), you will also need for this project a piece of blue handmade paper, and three pieces of tissue paper in mid blue, green and white. For the base use a piece of lightweight cotton or muslin stretched in a hoop.

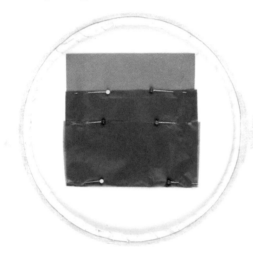

1 Assemble the papers you have selected to create a collage base on the lightweight cotton or muslin stretched in a hoop. These will form the basis for your stitching. Cut or tear off each piece about 13cm (5in) wide (the width of the finished embroidery). Here I have used a piece of blue handmade paper for the sky, mid blue tissue paper for the distant sea and green tissue paper for the foreground sea. Pin the papers in place, starting with the sky and overlapping them. The blue tissue should continue beneath the green to the base of the picture.

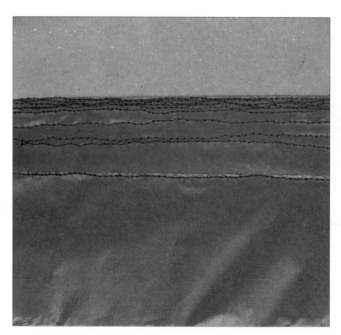

2 Put dark blue thread on the top of the machine and a slightly lighter shade in the bobbin. Run a line of small straight stitches just below the horizon line. Take the stitching up and along the top of the sky to hold it in place, then stitch along the top and bottom edges of the green paper. The lines of stitching at the top and bottom of the picture will eventually be hidden under the mount.

3 Using slightly meandering lines, work rows of stitching from the horizon down to just below the middle of the central blue panel, increasing the distance between them as you move forwards.

4 Put the lighter blue thread on top of the machine as well as in the bobbin and work rows of straight stitch in between the previous stitching, taking them down to the bottom of the blue panel. As before, work with slightly wavy lines to give the impression of gentle background waves.

5 Pin a length of crumpled white tissue paper on to the background to represent a foaming wave.

6 With bright white thread on the top of the machine and in the bobbin, stitch down the tissue paper. Use small, spiralling movements of the hoop and stitch over the paper, taking some of the stitching above and below the paper to look like foam. Avoid stitching over the tissue paper too densely in order to retain the crumpled, textured look.

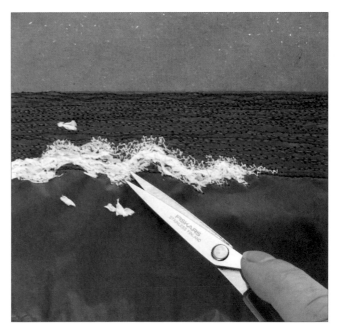

7 Scratch away some of the tissue paper using the points of a pair of scissors, revealing the blue paper underneath. If you scratch away too much paper, fill the unwanted gaps either with small pieces of tissue paper stitched into place, or with stitching alone.

8 Put light blue thread on top and white in the bobbin and define the shape of the wave using curved, diagonal lines of straight stitching. Tighten the top tension to pull up the bobbin thread every now and then and use tiny stitches to suggest floating foam.

9 With dark blue thread in the bobbin and on the top of the machine, stitch more curved lines in straight stitch at the top of the wave and under the base of the white foam to create a shadow.

10 For the floating foam on the water in front of the wave, use bright white thread on the top and in the bobbin and stitch horizontal lines of small straight stitches worked in shallow curves. Some of the green tissue will be broken up by the stitching, revealing the blue tissue underneath. Concentrate mainly on the left-hand side of the picture.

11 Tear up some pieces of black handmade paper and pin them to the background to represent rocks.

12 Continue the white stitching around the bases of the rocks to anchor them in place and remove the pins.

13 Lay on some crumpled white tissue paper to represent the foaming waves breaking on the rocks. Pin the pieces of paper in place. It is better to use more paper than you need, as the excess can be torn off once the paper has been stitched down.

14 With bright white thread top and bottom, work spiralling lines of straight stitching amongst the foam. Increase the stitch length and work horizontal lines of stitching in the water in front of the rocks to resemble floating foam. Work more stitches where you want a denser white, for example around the base of the rocks.

15 Scratch away some of the white tissue paper to create texture in the waves. Notice the flecks of blue in the foreground – this is the blue tissue paper showing through the green. The stitches have broken up the green paper to reveal the blue underneath.

Project: Pebble Beach

A cold, windy day at the beach. With weather conditions better for windsurfers than sunbathers, the dramatic waves more than made up for it and I got some great photographs for inspiration.

The two source photographs for this project gave me a starting point, a composition, a tonal range and detail reference, though my thread choices were more from memory than from accurately matching them to the photos. Having made a sketch of my design, I gathered together the threads I needed and wound some bobbins ready with the base colours.

You will need

Source photographs and sketches for inspiration, colour and detail reference
Medium-weight white habutai silk for the painted background
Wooden frame on which to stretch the silk
Silk pins
Air/water-soluble pen
Resist in a pen with a nib
Embroidery hoop
Embroidery scissors
Sewing machine
Silk paints and brushes
Water pot
Iron to fix the paints
A range of threads and bobbins

1 Transfer the design on to your silk by either tracing or drawing freehand from the sketch. Paint the main elements, then wash the silk and fix the paints (see pages 28–29).

I took elements from each of the two photographs and composed the portrait-format picture shown in the sketch on the left. The final embroidery measures 10 x 18cm (4 x 7in) so if you are using the same sketch as the one shown here, you will need to reproduce it at approximately 140 per cent.

2 Stretch the silk in a 20cm (8in) bound hoop. You will start with the background sea and headland, so make sure these lie completely within the frame.

3 Thread the machine with off-white on the top and mid green in the bobbin and work very small straight stitches in a 'two stitches forwards, one stitch back' motion for the small area of rough sea towards the back of the picture. The most distant part of the sea will remain unstitched to create depth.

4 With black thread on the top and in the bobbin, use straight stitch to lay dark stitching over the darkest parts of the rocky headland in the distance. Use small stitches to give a sense of depth to the picture, and work them in short, jagged, diagonal lines to mimic the shapes and forms within the rocks. Lay denser stitching at the base of the rocks where they are darker, and leave more gaps in the stitching higher up. Leave the small rock nearest the foreground unstitched.

Here are some of the threads and loaded bobbins that I used for this project. Add in more colours as your embroidery progresses, and take out any you decide simply don't work.

5 Leave black thread in the bobbin and put dark grey on the top. Fill in the gaps left higher up on the rocks where they are lighter, overlapping some of the previous stitching to blend in the colour. This gives some highlights to the headland.

6 Place dark blue-green in the bobbin and a mid blue-green on the top and stitch the area of choppy water just in front of the headland. Use the technique of two stitches forwards, one stitch back worked in horizontal lines. Avoid the small, unstitched rock nearest the foreground. Increase the length of the stitches slightly as you move forwards to give a sense of depth and perspective.

Tip

You might find it easier to stitch straight, horizontal lines by turning the hoop through 90° and moving it up and down rather than from side to side.

7 Leave the same colour on the top of the machine and put off-white in the bobbin. Adjust the top tension to pull up a fleck of white and stitch amongst the previous stitching in horizontal lines.

8 For the small rock, work diagonal straight stitches using dark grey on the top and black in the bobbin. Working the rock after the sea behind it makes it stand out and pushes the sea further into the foreground.

9 Move towards the foreground and, with mid blue-green in the bobbin and on the top, work straight stitch in diagonal lines to indicate the swell of the first wave. Leave gaps in between the stitching.

10 Put a very pale blue thread on top and off-white in the bobbin and stitch in between the previous lines of stitching to suggest foam. Work the stitching more densely along the top of the wave. Overlap the base of the small rock to set if firmly in place within the picture.

11 Moving now into the next wave, work the dark patches first with dark green thread on top and mid green in the bobbin. Use straight stitch and work at a slight angle to produce small, dark patches using the 'two stitches forwards, one stitch back' technique. Remember to refer to the photograph for shape and colour.

12 With a very pale blue thread on top and in the bobbin, use a slightly longer stitch and work in between the dark green patches. Keep the overall look of this area relatively flat and smooth. Work denser stitching along the top of the wave and the base of the headland.

13 Put off-white in the bobbin and tighten the top tension to pull up the bobbin thread. Work the highlights along the top of the wave using tiny straight stitches. Fill in any remaining gaps within the wave itself and make sure you overlap the base of the headland with these colours.

14 Leave off-white in the bobbin and put black on the top, and stitch the spray thrown up at the base of the rocks. Make sure the top tension is still tight. The black thread will blend into the rocks and the bobbin thread will appear as white dots of spray.

15 Add highlights to the top edges of the rocks using mid grey in the bobbin and light grey on the top of the machine.

16 Put dark green on the top and dark blue-green in the bobbin and work the shaded areas on the underside of the main wave in the foreground. Start at the base of the wave and take the stitching up towards the top, following the curve of the wave. Continue along the base, avoiding the front of the wave as this will be stitched later.

17 Change the colour on the top of the machine to mid green and put in the lighter tones higher up on the underside of the wave. Work in between the previous lines of stitching, overlapping them slightly to blend the colours.

18 With the same thread colours, work some spiralling stitching into the front of the wave and along the front edge. Concentrate the stitching just above the lines of foam that you drew on in resist.

19 Put the mid green in the bobbin and a very pale blue on the top and move the hoop in a spiralling motion to stitch the foam on the front of the wave.

20 With the same thread colours, put in the floating foam on the underside of the wave in curved lines. Take some of the stitching down to the bottom of the wave in long, slender, curved lines and lay the shorter stitch lines in a band across the top of the wave.

21 With bright white thread on top and very pale blue in the bobbin, put the highlights on the top of the wave. Use small, short, jagged stitch lines on the left-hand side of the wave, and tightly spiralling stitch lines on the right-hand part of the wave that is breaking on to the shore.

22 Moving forwards to the area of relatively calm water in front of the wave, use mid blue-green on the top of the machine and in the bobbin to put in the dark areas. Work horizontal lines of straight stitching from side to side across the picture (turn the hoop through 90° and move it up and down if you find this easier). Also put in the shadows within the foaming edge at the front of the water using small, spiralling movements of the hoop.

23 Put in the highlights on the water using very pale blue thread in the bobbin and bright white on the top of the machine. Create a longer stitch length by moving the hoop more quickly and work backwards and forwards in between the previous stitching so that it floats on top of it. Use spiralling stitch lines for the foam at the leading edge.

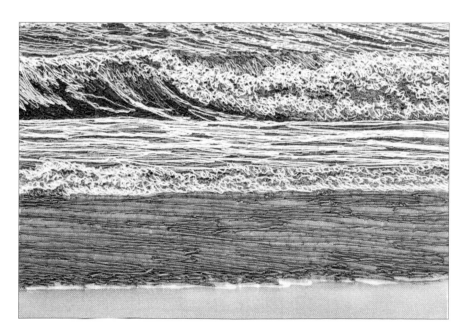

24 Moving forwards again, put mid grey on the top and in the bobbin and work a dense layer of horizontal stitching on the area of shallow water where the beach shows through and the colour changes noticeably from blue-green to grey.

69

25 Lay the floating foam on top of the water using off-white thread on top of the machine and very pale blue in the bobbin. Work in between the previous stitching using a slightly longer stitch so that the foam appears to sit on top of the water. Angle the hoop at 45° and work very small zigzag stitches along the front edge.

26 Moving forwards to the shallower water, use mid grey top and bottom and begin by laying a narrow band of straight stitches just under the foaming edge of the previous stitching.

27 Put a light grey-brown thread on the top of the machine to blend with the painted background, and very pale blue in the bobbin. Work widely spaced lines of straight stitching across the area using jerky movements of the hoop (three stitches forwards, one stitch back) to create texture.

28 With mid grey thread in the bobbin and light brown on top, start to put in the more distant pebbles using tiny, horizontal straight stitches. As you move towards the foreground, change to the 'two stitches forwards, one stitch back' technique to introduce a little more texture. Start to space out the stitching more as you move forwards to leave gaps for other colours.

29 Leave the same colour on the top of the machine and put a slightly darker grey in the bobbin. Stitch into the gaps left in the previous stitching then continue into the foreground using the same technique.

30 As you approach the foreground, change to very small zigzag stitches. Work the smaller individual pebbles by holding the hoop in one position so that the stitches build up on top of each other. Work in horizontal lines, and gradually widen the zigzag stitch as you move forwards to form larger pebbles. In the foreground, vary the angle at which you hold the hoop so that the stitching lies in different directions.

Tip

Leave some of the background colour showing through the stitching as this will resemble wet sand, but don't leave too many gaps otherwise the embroidery will look unfinished.

31 Place a warm, sandy brown thread on top of the machine and work more pebbles in between the previous ones. Continue to work in horizontal lines.

32 Change the bobbin colour to a very dark grey and put light brown on the top. Work more pebbles towards the front of the picture. This gives three different colours of pebbles mixed in together.

33 With a very dark brown in the bobbin and mid grey on top, work lines of straight stitching between the pebbles, concentrating on the foreground area. This will give the picture a sense of depth and cohesion. The slower you move the hoop, the more of the dark brown thread will be visible.

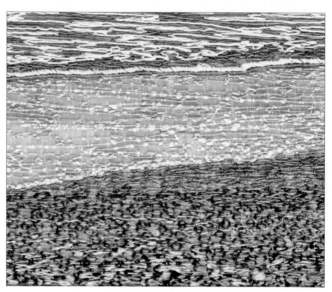

34 With off-white thread in the bobbin and mid grey on top, put in the line of foam at the edge of the water, where it meets the pebbles. Use straight stitching worked in small, spiralling movements of the hoop. Take some of the stitching up into the water to blend it in.

35 Put bright white thread on top and in the bobbin and strengthen the line of foam using small zigzag stitches. Take some of the stitching into the water behind to blend it in and make the stitches wider as you move towards the foreground.

36 Soften the grey area just in front of the blue-green sea using mid grey on top and off-white in the bobbin. Work through the existing stitching using straight stitches to lessen the contrast.

Pebble Beach

Original size 10 x 18cm (4 x 7in)

To finish, I decided to soften the pebbles at the water's edge with a small wave sinking rapidly into the pebbles. I stitched a sparse layer of horizontal straight stitches over them using bright white thread on top of the machine and mid grey in the bobbin. To obtain the foaming edge I worked slowly across the picture using small zigzag stitches.

Project: Crashing Wave

I took a lot of photographs to capture this huge wave at the right moment. I was fascinated by the dark, curving underbelly breaking into foam and spray at its maximum height.

I decided the background rock was too dominant and changed the shape of it to open up the sky and distant sea, giving more depth to the picture.

You will need

Source photographs and sketches for inspiration, colour and detail reference

Medium-weight white habutai silk for the painted background

Wooden frame on which to stretch the silk

Silk pins

Air/water-soluble pen

Resist in a pen with a nib

Embroidery hoop

Embroidery scissors

Sewing machine

Silk paints and brushes

Water pot

Iron to fix the paints

A range of threads and bobbins

The source photograph can simply be traced or copied on to the silk, with the modifications to the background rock described above. The final embroidery measures 18 x 13cm (7 x 5in) so if you are using the same photograph as the one shown here, you will need to reproduce it at approximately 160 per cent.

1 Transfer the design on to your silk by either tracing or copying the source photograph. Paint the main elements, then iron the silk to fix the dyes, wash it to remove the resist, and iron it once more (see pages 28–29).

2 Stretch the silk in a 20cm (8in) bound hoop. You will start with the background rocks, so make sure all of these lie within the frame.

3 With black in the bobbin and dark grey on top of the machine, set the machine to straight stitch and adjust the tension so that the bobbin thread is visible on the surface but is not too loose.

4 Using a small stitch length and moving the hoop slowly, work diagonal stitching across the rocks, following the direction of the rock strata. Don't stitch too densely, as further stitching will be laid on top. Move the hoop slightly from side to side as you work to avoid lines that are too straight, and vary the length of the stitches by altering the speed with which you move the hoop. Make sure you stitch over the white lines at the edges of the rocks.

Here are some of the threads and loaded bobbins that I used for this project.

Tip

Areas with smaller stitches will have a higher concentration of the darker 'dots' of bobbin thread, so use these where you want to achieve a slightly darker colour, for example at the base of the rock next to the sea.

5 Put the grey thread from the top of the machine in the bobbin and a mid grey on the top. (Transferring the colour from the top to the bobbin and only introducing one colour at a time help the colours to blend.)

6 Using the same technique as before, fill in some of the spaces.

Tip

The smaller the stitches at this stage, the more easily they will blend in with the previous stitching; the larger they are, the more they will stand out. Avoid over-working – the dark painted background ensures the gaps in the stitching won't show.

7 In preparation for working on the wave, move the position of the fabric in the hoop if necessary so that the entire wave lies within the frame. Mark on the lines of dark shading using an air/water-soluble pen, following the photograph for reference.

8 Put dark blue-green thread in the bobbin and a mid blue-green on the top of the machine and put in the dark rows of shading running through the wave, following the drawn lines. Use medium-length straight stitches, and keep the stitch length constant for a smooth effect.

9 Keep the same colour on the top of the machine and and put it in the bobbin too. Add in more stitching lines, taking them a little higher up the wave to help with blending.

10 Keep the same colour thread in the bobbin and put a lighter tone of blue-green on the top of the machine. Add more stitching lines, taking them a little higher again. Continue to follow the shape of the wave.

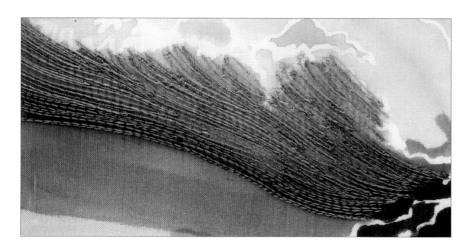

11 With the same colour on the top of the machine, this time put a greener tone in the bobbin. Introduce this colour higher up on the wave, following the shape of the wave as before.

Tip
By introducing only one new colour on the machine at a time, the colours will blend and merge more smoothly.

12 Put the same green that is in the bobbin on the top of the machine and fill in the top of the wave.

Tip

When working the underside of the wave, keep all the stitches the same length as this will produce a smooth effect.

13 Now work on the crest of the wave, where it tumbles forwards. Put in the darkest patches first, following the lines marked in resist on the silk and referring to the source photograph. Start with two mid blue-greens and put the darker one in the bobbin.

14 Still using straight stitch, work curved lines, following the shape of the wave.

Tip

Work the crest of the wave using a generous amount of stitches as some of them will be partly covered with further stitching when you add the sea spray.

15 With the darker tone on the top of the machine as well as in the bobbin, put in the darker tones towards the left-hand side of the wave. Also put a little of the darker colour in amongst the previous stitching for a more coherent finish.

Tip

When filling areas with several different coloured stitches, intermingle them slightly so that the colours blend together.

16 For the mid tones, use a mid blue-green in the bobbin and a pale blue on the top. Look for the lighter areas and stitch through them, overlapping some of the previous stitching to blend in the colours. Continue to follow the shape of the wave.

17 Start to put in the foam. Use off-white thread on the top and a very pale blue in the bobbin. Continue to use straight stitch, but move the hoop in a spiralling motion to create the texture of frothy foam.

18 Work into the gaps in the previous stitching, using the photograph and the white lines drawn on the silk for reference. Take some of the stitching a little above the wave where it splashes up in front of the rocks.

> ### Tip
> You need to identify the abstract shapes in the photograph in order to produce the same effect in stitch. Sometimes, turning the photograph upside-down can help with this.

19 Soften the white foam a little by putting the off-white in the bobbin and a mid blue-green on the top. Tighten the top tension to pull up the bobbin thread and work a meandering line of straight stitching over the edges of the foam to blend it in with the rest of the wave.

> ### Tip
> Pulling up the white bobbin thread will create texture, and the blue-green top thread will blend in with the rest of the stitching and create a more muted overall effect.

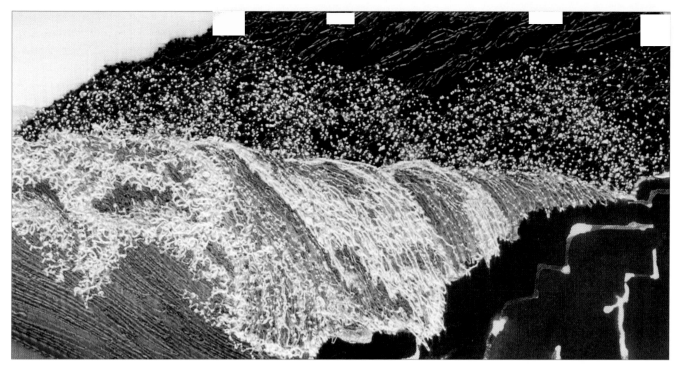

20 For the spray laying over the distant rocks, keep the off-white in the bobbin and put a dark grey on top. Make sure the bobbin thread is pulled up and work a meandering stitch line over the lower part of the rocks. Avoid taking the stitching into the water – stop at the top of the wave.

Tip

This will create quite a subtle, misty spray. Rather than making it too dense at this stage, re-assess it when more of the picture has been worked and, if necessary, strengthen it then.

21 Return to the main wave and, with dark blue-green in the bobbin and mid blue on top, work the base of the wave. Use medium-length straight stitches, as you did before, and work in smooth lines, following the curve of the wave. Take some of stitching up into the lighter part of the wave to blend it in.

22 Put a pale grey in the bobbin and on the top and put in the pale grey patches of reflected light at the bottom of the wave, using straight stitch as before.

23 Change to a mid grey thread top and bottom and put some slightly darker patches a little higher up. Continue to follow the shape of the wave with your stitching.

24 With dark blue-green top and bottom, run this darker stitching between the blocks of grey to separate them out and give them more definition.

25 Add the floating foam at the bottom of the picture. Keep the dark blue-green thread in the bobbin and put a slightly lighter blue-green on the top and lay a foundation of fairly dense horizontal straight stitches just below the bottom of the wave. Take some of the stitching lines out to the right to create the darker patches in the water.

26 Put bright white thread on the top of the machine and off-white in the bobbin. Work the area of foam just to the left of the foreground rock. Work in a 'two stitches forwards, one stitch back' motion, backwards and forwards across the embroidery, to build up a dense layer of stitching.

27 Moving now to the foreground rock, put in the darker sections using dark grey thread on the top of the machine and black in the bobbin. Use straight stitching worked mostly in vertical but also in horizontal lines, and follow the shapes and contours of the rocks. Build up a dense layer of stitching, using longer stitches for the lighter areas and shorter stitches for the darker ones.

28 Put the dark grey thread in the bobbin and a lighter grey on the top. Identify the lighter areas of the rocks from the photograph (these will be the highlights) and stitch them using the same technique. Try to avoid stitching over the white lines on the fabric. These indicate where the water is flowing over the rocks, which is stitched later.

29 Move the light grey thread from the top to the bobbin and put a very pale blue on the top for the water trickling down the rocks. Use small straight stitches and 'wiggle' the hoop as you work to produce wavy lines of stitching. Pick out the less bright areas of water first.

30 Change to bright white thread on top and off-white in the bobbin and put in the brighter tumbling water. Move the hoop in a spiralling motion to produce texture.

31 Add the fragmented dots of spray by using dark grey on the top and bright white in the bobbin. Tighten the top tension to pull up the bobbin thread and work lines of stitching, using the photograph for reference. The dark grey top thread will blend in with the rock, leaving just the dots of white bobbin thread visible.

32 Using the same threads and the same technique, strengthen the lower part of the spray on the distant rocks. Move the hoop slowly so that the stitches are small and the dots nearly touching each other. Avoid stitching into the wave.

> **Tip**
>
> Emphasising the spray in the background will make the foreground rock stand out more.

33 Move the hoop and work on the water at the base of the foreground rock. Put mid grey on the top of the machine and dark grey in the bobbin and adjust the top tension so that the bobbin thread lies flat. Using horizontal straight stitches, lay in the dark areas underneath the foam.

34 Put bright white thread on the top of the machine and off-white in the bobbin and stitch the floating foam on the surface of the water in the foreground. Hold the hoop so that the picture is the right way up and work zigzag stitches across the embroidery in horizontal lines. Leave a few small patches of grey visible. Hold the hoop still every now and then and allow the stitches to build up on top of each other to create areas of texture and depth of stitch.

35 Strengthen the whites in the wave using bright white thread on top and in the bobbin. Work in straight stitch and move the hoop in a spiralling motion, referring to the photograph for guidance on where to place the stitching.

36 Finally, put some dots of white foam on the wave using pale blue in the bobbin and dark blue-green on the top of the machine. Use straight stitch with the bobbin thread pulled up. Work in curved lines using irregular lengths of stitches to achieve a random distribution of dots, and use the photograph for reference.

Crashing Wave

Original size 18 x 13cm (7 x 5in)

When an embroidery is near completion, I stand back from it and assess the colours, shapes and tones I have used and make sure everything is progressing well. Placing the embroidery, the photographs and sketches upside down can be really helpful here. After some consideration I thought this picture needed more tonal contrast. I changed the bobbin colour to dark blue-green and added a few curved lines in the base of the wave for a little more definition. I strengthened the white in the wave using bright white on top and in the bobbin and worked in straight stitch, moving the hoop in a spiralling motion. Finally, with the same thread colours, I added even more spray at the top of the wave in front of the background rock.

Project: Splash!

Clambering over the rocks is worth all the effort when I get to see and be inspired by scenes like this. Waiting for the splash in the heat of the day, with the intensity of the deep blue sea stretching before me, I imagine how all I can see will be interpreted in paint and stitch. This scene gives a rich, intense colour palette with the contrast of the textured, white spray. The thread colours are a range of strong blues and greens for the sea and browns for the rocks.

You will need

Source photographs and sketches for inspiration, colour and detail reference
Medium-weight white habutai silk for the painted background
Wooden frame on which to stretch the silk
Silk pins
Air/water-soluble pen
Resist in a pen with a nib
Embroidery hoop
Embroidery scissors
Sewing machine
Silk paints and brushes
Water pot
Iron to fix the paints
A range of threads and bobbins

I wanted to create a square composition from a landscape-format photograph, so I decided to crop off the left-hand side to bring the 'splash' further into the middle of the picture, but retained the distant mountains. The final embroidery measures 13 x 13cm (5 x 5in) so if you are using the same photograph as the one shown here, you will need to reproduce it at 160 per cent.

1 Transfer the design on to your silk by either tracing or copying the source photograph.

2 To obtain a graduated sky, mix three shades of blue silk paint and apply one after the other in horizontal strokes, starting with the palest at the horizon. Allow the colours to blend naturally on the silk. The sea will be covered in stitching and can therefore be painted more simply using the darkest blue. Add a little green to the mix for the part of the sea nearest the foreground, and dab a lighter version of the same mix in the area behind the spray. Mix a dark brown using brown and black for the rocks. Paint the distant mountains and greenery freehand once the sky is dry using pale mixes of muted browns and greens and a small brush. Use the source photograph for reference.

3 Fix the paints with a hot iron and wash the silk (see pages 28–29).

4 Stretch the silk in a 20cm (8in) bound hoop. Make sure the top tension is tight enough to pull up the bobbin thread and start to stitch on the horizon. Put dark blue in the bobbin and a slightly lighter blue on the top of the machine. Work in straight stitch, using small, uniform stitches to achieve a flat, even finish. Keep the lines of stitching as straight as possible and bring the colour forwards a little into the sea.

Tip
You might find it easier to stitch straight, horizontal lines by turning the hoop through 90° and moving it up and down rather than from side to side.

A selection of the threads and loaded bobbins that I used for this project.

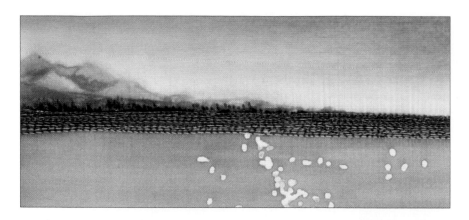

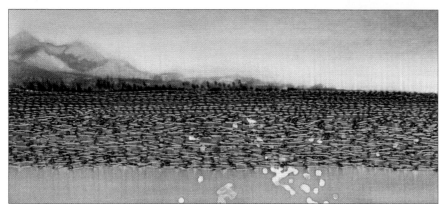

5 Leave the same thread in the bobbin and put a slightly lighter thread on the top. Continue the stitching further down the picture, making the stitches slightly larger by moving the hoop quicker.

Tip

To blend areas more effectively, avoid changing both the colours and the techniques you are using at the same time.

6 Using the same thread colours, change the technique slightly to 'two stitches forwards, one stitch back' and bring the stitching further forwards, where the sea becomes more choppy. Increase the stitch length slightly as you move further forwards and avoid over-stitching – allow the background colour to show through.

7 Leave the same colour in the bobbin and put a very dark blue on the top. Continue with the 'two forwards, one back' technique and lay in the dark lines of stitching. Leave large gaps between the lines of stitching – these will be filled with further layers of stitches later.

Tip

If you are still working with your hoop at 90°, remember to turn the source photograph sideways too.

8 Leave the same colour in the bobbin and put a pale blue on top and run the lighter stitching amongst the dark blue, overlapping the colours slightly. Take the lighter colour up into the choppy water in the middle distance to blend the colours. Continue with the 'two forwards, one backwards' technique, increasing the stitch length slightly as you move forwards into the foreground and decreasing it as you move backwards. Leave gaps in the stitching so that further colours can be introduced later.

9 Replace the top thread with jade green and work the colour in between the dark blue. Bring the stitching further into the foreground as well as a little into the background to blend it in. Remember to reduce the size of the stitches as you work further backwards.

10 The sea colour on the left of the spray is slightly more subdued. Put a mid teal blue thread on the top of the machine and work this area using the same technique as before (two stitches forwards, one stitch back). Put a little of this colour on the right too to link the areas together.

11 Replace the teal blue with a slightly paler version and lay further stitching in between the previous stitching on the left-hand side. This will break up the colour and make it a little lighter. Put some of this colour on the right too, and take it into the stitching higher up to blend it in. Work one or two small patches into the spray itself, using small, spiralling movements of the hoop. At the bottom of the picture on the left the sea is less choppy, so use curved lines of straight stitch here rather than the 'two forwards, one back' technique.

12 Put a very dark grey-green on top and in the bobbin and lay dark stitching in the sea at the very front of the picture, just behind the rocks. This will create contrast when you start stitching the foam. Use straight stitches worked in curved lines.

13 Replace the top thread with dark green and add in a little green here and there in the foreground areas of the sea to fill in the gaps and give the water a subtle green tinge.

14 Put the floating foam on the left using a very pale blue-grey in the bobbin as well as on the top of the machine. Identify the shapes made by the foam in the photograph and work 'two stitches forwards, one stitch back' using fairly long stitches.

15 With the same colour in the bobbin and off-white on the top, make the foam a little brighter. Use the same technique to work the lighter stitching in between the lines of foam already worked.

16 Put mid grey thread on top of the machine and in the bobbin, and work spiralling straight stitches into the shadows within the spray. Run a little of the same colour into the floating foam on the left too.

17 With off-white thread in the bobbin and bright white on the top of the machine, start to put in the lightest parts of the spray. Identify the shapes in the photograph and use these as reference. Work in tiny zigzag stitches and move the hoop very slowly in meandering lines so that the stitches build up on top of each other. Work within the main body of the spray, varying the stitch width slightly and overlapping the grey stitching to blend it in.

18 For the finer splashes and isolated dots of foam at the edge of the spray, work several zigzag stitches in one spot and then move on to the next.

19 With the same two blues that you used on the horizon (dark blue in the bobbin and a slightly lighter blue on the top), work horizontal straight stitches in between the individual dots of foam to isolate them. The blue stitching will blend into the background and become invisible.

20 Put a very dark brown in the bobbin and a slightly lighter brown on the top. Use diagonal lines of straight stitching to put in the dark areas on the rocks.

21 Move the top colour to the bobbin and use a slightly lighter shade on the top to stitch the lighter parts of the rocks. Vary the line length but keep the stitch length the same.

22 Once again, put the top colour in the bobbin and a lighter shade on the top and place a few highlights on the rocks, using the photograph for reference.

23 With dark blue on the top of the machine and a slightly lighter blue in the bobbin, stitch into the spray on the right-hand side of the picture to break it up and give it a less pronounced outline. Change the top thread to mid teal blue and stitch into the spray at the top and on the left-hand side.

24 With bright white thread on the top and in the bobbin, put in the specks of spray that are covering the sky. Use the same technique that you used before (zigzag stitches worked on top of each other before moving on to the next dot), varying the sizes of the dots and the angle of the hoop to get a more random effect. Cut the connecting threads between the dots of spray against the sky.

Splash!

Original size 13 x 13cm (5 x 5in)

To finish this piece, I stitched into the grey floating foam on the left to break it up a little and push it into the background. I used a dark blue in the bobbin and mid teal blue on the top and worked in small, horizontal stitches. I worked some more small zigzags into the splash, rotating the hoop so they sat at various different angles to the horizontal, adding to the texture and impact of this focal point.

Index

Gazing out to Sea

Original size 6.5 x 10cm (2½ x 4in)

A small, simplified study of a calm sea, encompassing a surprising number of colours.